W9-CLU-765

5/24
STRAND PRICE
$5.00

AB.0171

to art with
love & prayers
f. zony
2004

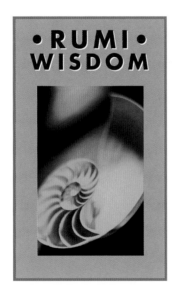

• RUMI •
WISDOM

• RUMI •
WISDOM

*Daily Teachings
from the Great
Sufi Master*

TIMOTHY FREKE

 A GODSFIELD BOOK

This book is dedicated to all those mad with love

First published in Great Britain in 2000
by Godsfield Press Ltd
A division of David and Charles Ltd
Laurel House, Station Approach,
New Alresford, Hants SO24 9JH, UK

10 9 8 7 6 5 4 3 2 1

© 2000 Godsfield Press
Text © Timothy Freke

Designed for Godsfield Press by
The Bridgewater Book Company

All rights reserved. No part of this publication may be reproduced,
stored in a retrieval system, or transmitted in any form or by any
means, electronic, mechanical, photocopying, recording, or otherwise.

Timothy Freke asserts the moral right to be
identified as the author of this work.

Printed and bound in China

ISBN 1-84181-024-X

Picture research: Caroline Thomas
Design: Alison Honey

The publishers wish to thank the following for the use of pictures:
The Stock Market (cover, pp. 1, 2, 3)
Sonia Halliday Photographs

CONTENTS

INTRODUCTION

"Lovers have a religion all of their own.
Their only creed is Love."

MEVLANA JALAL AL-DIN RUMI

Who was Mevlana Jalal al-Din Rumi? He would have been the first to laugh out loud at the impossibility of ever really answering this question. Rumi spent his life looking for Rumi. When he finally found him, he concluded that he didn't exist. Rumi is a paradoxical conundrum. He is a religious teacher who taught that all spiritual philosophies are inadequate. He is a great poet who regarded poetry as trifling entertainment. He is a sophisticated scholar who delighted in colloquial jokes. He is a teetotaler who wrote enthusiastically about drunkenness. He is a narrator of fables who saw himself as a fictional character. He is a venerated sage who regarded himself as a devil. He is a mortal man who claimed to be God incognito.

Rumi is famous as a Sufi poet. The Sufis are Islamic mystics. Their doctrines are practically indistinguishable from those of other mystical traditions. This has led to the claim that Sufism is a syncretic mix of Islam, Hinduism, Neo-platonic Paganism, and Christian Gnosticism. These traditions influenced the Sufis, but this doesn't mean that Sufism is a later deviation from the original Islam of Muhammad. Although they have often found themselves horribly persecuted by orthodox Muslim authorities, the Sufis see themselves as maintaining the genuine Islamic tradition. They claim to possess secret mystical teachings handed down through a line of enlightened Masters from the Prophet himself.

Rumi was born in 1207 in Balkh in what today is Afghanistan. At an early age, his family settled in Turkey. His father was a well-respected Sufi teacher and author of a mystical treatise called *Gnosis* or "Mystical Knowledge." As a boy, Rumi is said to have met with many Sufi Masters, including the great Farid al-Din Attar, who gave him a copy of his *Book of Secrets* – a powerful mystical poem from which Rumi often quoted in later life. Attar immediately recognized Rumi's greatness. As the child left with his illustrious father, he commented, "There goes a river dragging an ocean behind it."

THE ARRIVAL OF THE WILDMAN

As an adult, Rumi acquired a prestigious reputation as a religious scholar and teacher. Then, in 1244, at the age of thirty-seven, his world was unexpectedly turned upside down. Into town came a wandering wildman from Tabriz called Shams al-Din. Shams was about sixty years old. He was a Sufi sage from the Shi'ite Ismaeli tradition of Islam, rather than the Sunni tradition in which Rumi had been brought up. Shams had spent his life in search of "The Hidden Iman" – the perfect enlightened sage. Some have interpreted this as a search for a man. But it is more likely that Shams himself interpreted this as the search for the Divine Teacher within, which the Hindus call the "Satguru" and the Gnostic Christians call "Christ."

Rumi was sober, devout, respectable, and influential. Shams was rude, forthright, unconventional, and on fire with devotion. Yet, when the two men met, they recognized in each other the same obsession with the great Mystery of Life. They fell into Love with each other and became inseparable. Shams was known as "Parindah" – "the flier." He had no respect for religious authorities or spiritual niceties. He wanted to fly. He threw all of Rumi's books into a fountain. Rumi abandoned his scholarly studies and stopped teaching his students.

Instead, he spent his time soaring to the heights of ecstasy with this mad old man. Was Shams Rumi's Master? Was Rumi Shams' "Hidden Iman"? Were they soul-friends who shared a sublime enthusiasm for Truth? Whatever their relationship, they were mirrors of each other's light.

And then, as suddenly as he had come, Shams left. Rumi was distraught. He sent his son to search for Shams and eventually he found him in Damascus playing chess. Despite Shams' indifference, he was eventually persuaded to return to Rumi, only to disappear once again in 1247 – this time without trace. Legend has it that he was murdered by some of Rumi's disciples, who were jealous of his influence on their Master. Maybe. Or perhaps he knew his job was complete and that Rumi would have to make the rest of his spiritual journey on his own?

The Rumi that Shams left behind was no longer the orthodox teacher he had once been. An uncontrollable torrent of poetry poured from his heart, unleashed by Shams. Rumi was not himself. Something deep and mysterious was speaking through him. He often signed his work "The Silent." On his mystical adventures into the depths of consciousness with Shams, he had learned to quiet the inner turmoil of his ego and become a passive echo of the Divine Word within.

Rumi's students no longer gathered to receive traditional teachings from a conservative scholar, but to be swept up in the whirlwind of his devotion. To the music of pipes and drums, they danced symbolic dances that Shams had taught Rumi, becoming known as the "The Whirling Dervishes." They thrilled to Rumi's ranting lyric love poetry, composed extempore on the spot and hastily recorded by one of his disciples. To convey the intensity of his mystical experiences, Rumi turned to dangerous and forbidden metaphors. Although Muslims were not allowed to drink alcohol, he writes of being intoxicated with bewildering ecstasy. To capture his passionate rapture, he uses images of romantic love. His love of God and his love of Shams merged to become one consuming obsession. All of his life became a love affair with his Beloved.

A TRACKLESS OCEAN

Rumi raved on until his death in 1273 at the age of sixty-six, leaving behind two great works of inspirational poetry – the *Diwan-i Shams-i-Tabriz*, dedicated to Shams, and the *Mathnawi-i-Maanawi*, or "Couplets of Inner Meaning" – as well as a prose work called the *Fihi ma fihi*, generally referred to as the *Discourses*. *Rumi Wisdom* contains extracts from his masterwork, the *Mathnawi*, which he began in his fifties and continued to compose until his death. It is a monumental poem of 25,700 verses – longer than the *Iliad* and the *Odyssey* combined!

The eminent Islamic scholar R.A. Nicholson described the *Mathnawi* as "a trackless ocean." It is rambling and anarchic in structure – a fascinating mixture of funny allegorical stories, profound insights, and intoxicated devotion. To attempt to condense this work into a coherent philosophy would be to turn a flamboyant bird singing in the trees into a dissected specimen pinned lifelessly in a museum display case. In his *Discourses*, Rumi

compares "reason" to a moth flying around a candle flame. It is drawn to the light of the Beloved, flying closer and closer until eventually it is consumed through communion. Rumi uses ideas to take us beyond ideas. He wants us to burn, not to think. To understand Rumi is to catch a feeling, not to understand a philosophical system.

In the *Mathnawi* he writes:

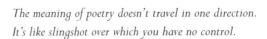

> *The meaning of poetry doesn't travel in one direction.*
> *It's like slingshot over which you have no control.*

Unlike prose, poetry by its very nature does not have a single meaning, but resonates in different ways for different listeners. This was its attraction for Rumi. Here was a form of communication that could speak on many levels at once. Listeners can take from his words what they are capable of understanding – from mild entertainment to sublime insight. The danger with organized teachings is that the student becomes trapped in a merely conceptual understanding of mysticism. Rumi's poetic insights, however, are too intangible for that. They are seeds from which more and more meaning grows over time, according to the nature of the ground they are planted in.

Today Rumi is routinely described as the greatest of all mystical poets. Yet he himself was dismissive of his poetry. What mattered to Rumi was not the words and form, but the sublime understanding from which they originated. In the *Discourses*, he explains:

> *I love the friends that come to me so much that, concerned they may get*
> *easily bored, I speak poetry to entertain them. Otherwise, poetry is of no*
> *concern to me. By Allah, I really couldn't give a damn about poetry. I can't*

think of anything less interesting. It has become necessary for me to be a poet, just as when a guest wants to eat tripe it is incumbent upon the host to feed him tripe.

As you feed further on the exotic bowl of tripe you are now reading, by all means let Rumi's words amuse you. But also reach beyond them to the hidden meaning, which they can only partly express. Let the words be signposts pointing away from themselves to an ineffable destination – an intuitive apprehension of Truth. Never forget that, although Rumi is an entertainer, he is first and foremost a sage.

DAILY INSPIRATION

In this book, I have presented extracts from the *Mathnawi* as easily accessible short poems or succinct insights. Employing the same technique I have used in my other comparable works, I have adapted a reliable literal translation of the original poem – in this case that of R.A. Nicholson. Despite its scholarly strengths, this translation is mystically and poetically inadequate and, therefore, in an important sense, misrepresents Rumi. There is, in my view, no such thing as a

genuine "literal" translation. Rendering the *Mathnawi* word-for-word may result in an accurate translation in one sense, but we do not hear Rumi's words as his original audience would have heard them. They sound like the safely old-fashioned lectures of a long-dead saint, not the dangerously in-your-face rantings of a living enigma! In this sense, such translations are inauthentic.

Trusting to Nicholson's skills as a linguist and my own lifelong experience of mysticism, I hope to have brought out the essence of Rumi's meaning in a thoroughly contemporary way. Where necessary, I have updated style, language,  and imagery, so that Rumi makes something of the same impact on our modern minds as he did upon his other students eight hundred years ago. I have done my best not to misrepresent Rumi or add too much of myself, but my work is necessarily an interpretation. I have selected only those parts of the *Mathnawi* that appeal to me, for which I make no apologies. Rumi is a medieval mystic, and sometimes he seems a distant figure from a remote culture. I am interested only in those moments when he speaks with a timeless voice, offering perennial wisdom — as alive now as it was in thirteenth-century Turkey.

The extracts are presented in a "thought-for-the-day" format, so that you can use each day's insight as a focus for meditation. Alternatively, you may simply breeze through the book in search of those moments that particularly touch you. However you approach this book, be sure not to rush over a poem that interests you. Read it again and again. The first time, it may get only as far as your head. It will probably take a little while before it sinks to your heart, and even longer before it finally falls down to your guts.

As this is a yearbook, I have gathered the extracts together in selections according to the seasons, using the circle of the year as a loose allegory for the mystical journey. Day by day, insight by insight, we are led on a remarkable mystical voyage of discovery. During *Spring*, we are introduced to the idea of the spiritual quest. During *Summer*, we celebrate the intoxicating highs of an encounter with the Beloved. During *Fall*, we face the harsh reality of separation from God and the awesome challenge of dying to self. During *Winter*, we discover life in death and drown in the ocean of Allah. Certain themes recur and develop as we make this yearly journey. Without wishing to corral Rumi's passion into making intellectual sense, let's briefly explore these essential ideas.

HE WHO KNOWS HIMSELF KNOWS GOD

Rumi's insights are the fruits of having made an experiential journey in search of Truth. For Rumi, this is the very purpose of life. In the *Discourses*, he explains:

> *There is one thing in this world which must never be forgotten. If you forget everything else, but remember this, there will be no cause for regret. But if you remember everything else, but forget this one thing, then you will have done nothing whatsoever. It is as if a king has sent you to a foreign country to carry out a specified task. If you go and perform a hundred other tasks, but not what you were sent there to do, you have accomplished nothing. In the same way, human beings have come into this world for a particular task, and if they don't perform it they will have done nothing.*

What is this task? It is to make the spiritual journey, to penetrate the Mysteries of Life and Death, to commune with God. But who or what is God? For the Sufis, God is the Oneness of all that is. He is the manifest and the Mystery. This is conveyed eloquently by the Islamic name for God – "Allah" – which combines the roots "al" and "la" to mean "The Oneness of Being and Nothingness." But Rumi does not treat God only as an abstract principle. God is his Beloved Friend. God is the power of Love inside the human heart.

Muhammad teaches "He who knows himself knows God." This is the essence of Rumi's Sufism. In the *Diwan* he writes, "I gazed into my own heart and there I found Him — nowhere else." God is our true identity. God is the animating Consciousness of the Universe and every being within it. There is only God. All separateness is an illusion, including the idea of ourselves as separate individuals. When we wake up from this dream, we will know that we are God in search of God. We are God in the process of coming to know Himself. As separate individuals, we are waves on the great ocean of Allah, which is our deeper identity. What appear to be our thoughts and acts are in reality the currents of the whole sea. In the *Discourses*, Rumi writes:

We are like a bowl floating on the surface of water. The movement of the bowl on the surface of the water is controlled not by the bowl but by the water. In the same way, the source of a person's actions is not that person but God.

How can we learn to embody this extraordinary understanding? Islam means "surrender." Like other Muslim mystics, Rumi teaches that, to become conscious of our Oneness with God, we must surrender our separate self to God. We must dissolve our separateness into his ocean of Love. Then we will experience "Gnosis," "mystical enlightenment," and become a "Gnostic," a "Knower."

For Rumi, however, enlightenment is not a destination we can arrive at. It is an ongoing process of evolution. This profound teaching is captured by a fascinating legend that records the first conversation between Rumi and Shams:

To test out Rumi's insight, Shams asked him, *"Who is greater — the Prophet Muhammad or the Sufi sage Bayazid?"*

Rumi answered: "Without doubt Muhammad."

Shams asked him, "Why do you say that? Muhammad said we can never truly know God, yet Bayazid proclaimed 'I am God'! Why is Muhammad the greater?"

Rumi explained: "Muhammad progressed through many states of realization. Each time he reached a new level of understanding, he begged forgiveness for his previous ignorance. Only the Prophet had the endurance to contemplate God in all his aspects at once — in abstraction purified of everything else, and in manifestation. He refused to remain caught in any one level of understanding. Bayazid, on the other hand, was carried away by his arrival at the first stage and, intoxicated by this achievement, went no further."

Rumi wants us to abandon ourselves to both the joys of mystical union and the suffering of separation as two necessary aspects of one extraordinary journey of spiritual evolution. He wants us to know that essentially we are God, yet to also be authentically human. Rumi is a paradox because life itself is paradoxical. Why doesn't Rumi make sense? Because the reality he wants us to glimpse doesn't make sense. It is an impossible union of opposites. Existence is an all-consuming Oneness expressing itself as an infinitely granular manyness. Rumi doesn't offer an organized body of teachings because then we might get stuck in one level of understanding only. He wants us to experience just how big the picture is. The good news is, "We are God." The bad news is, "We are also the Devil." Like all good jokes, the Truth is delightfully ironic.

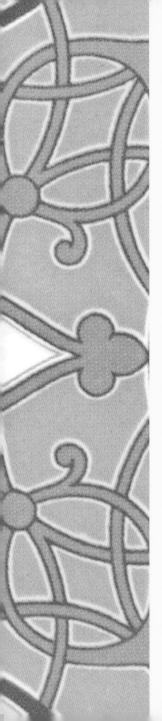

SPRING

MILK FROM THE NIPPLE
OF THE SOUL

Spring is the time for growth. Do you want to grow? Then suck on these teachings, as if they were your mother's breast. Follow their sweet scent to the Garden of Joy. Don't resign yourself to a lifetime of confinement in this prison of a world. Freedom exists for those willing to keep evolving. Clean your soul-mirror until it reflects the Light. Don't wear worn-out second-hand opinions. Know for yourself. Don't chase shadows. Embrace the Mystery. Don't just admire the jug. Drink the water. Spend your time wisely, before you're condemned as a bankrupt. Don't wait for tomorrow. Tomorrow has never existed and never will. Right now is all. Dive into the River of Transformation and swim to the Ocean of Allah.

MARCH

These teachings are milk from the nipple of the soul.
They won't flow well unless you suck.

MARCH

The garden of the heart is moist and fresh,
with jasmines, roses, and cypress trees.

My words carry their aroma.
Follow the scent to Eden.

MARCH

Don't get a house in the neighborhood of despair.
There is hope.

Don't drive off into the darkness.
There is light.

4

MARCH

Head out to sea —
even if your own mother
tells you to be afraid of the water.

You are a wild swan —
not some domestic fowl
to be kept in a stinking coop.

5

MARCH

The world is a prison exercise yard.
Head this way, where there's open country.

Appearances are the prison walls
which keep out that Reality.

6

MARCH

Stir like an embryo.
Evolve senses which can witness Light.
Mature in this womb-world,
and prepare for your second birth
out of earth into the limitless.

7

MARCH

What if someone said to an embryo in the womb,
"Outside of your world of black nothing
is a miraculously ordered universe;
a vast Earth covered with tasty food;
mountains, oceans, and plains,
fragrant orchards and fields full of crops;
a luminous sky beyond your reach,
with a sun, moonbeams, and uncountable stars;
and there are winds from south, north, and west,
and gardens replete with sweet flowers
like a banquet at a wedding feast.
The wonders of this world are beyond description.
What are you doing living in a dark prison,
drinking blood through that narrow tube?"
But the womb-world is all an embryo knows
and it would not be particularly impressed
by such amazing tales, saying dismissively:
"You're crazy. That is all a deluded fantasy."

MARCH

You have lived for lifetime after lifetime as a piece of rock.
Then somehow you became a plant and forgot about all that.
You then lived for lifetime after lifetime as a plant.
Then somehow you became an animal and forgot about all that.
You then lived for lifetime after lifetime as an animal.
Then somehow you became a human being.
You have completely changed state countless times already.
Do you really think you have now arrived
at the end of your evolution?

MARCH

Since your eyesight is evidently flawed,
why not try your insight?

Trade seeing for being – that's a great deal!
Then you'll get what you really want.

MARCH

Intuition is a foreign language to the ego.

11

MARCH

Hey! Mr Bribe-taker, don't you know
Spirit is the sweetener you are looking for?
It is the essence of sweetness.
Everything is sour without a sweet Spirit.

Eating honey makes you feel sweet,
but what are you going to do when the honey runs out?
Embrace Love and become honey.

12

MARCH

If you want to stop feeling perplexed,
stop stuffing cotton wool in your spiritual ears.
Then you might solve the riddle of form and meaning.

13

MARCH

Don't worry.
When they reach the Heart-Master,
even jagged rocks become jewels.

14

MARCH

You have sold out too cheaply.
You're satin sewn onto a tatty old raincoat.

15

MARCH

One day you will look back and laugh at yourself.
You'll say, "I can't believe I was so asleep!
How did I ever forget the truth?
How ridiculous to believe that sadness and sickness
are anything other than bad dreams."

MARCH

The reason you can't see
is that your soul-mirror
is armored with rust.

MARCH

You learned a trade to make a living
to keep body and soul together.
Now you need to learn a spiritual trade.
You've become well-clothed and wealthy here.
But how are you going to support yourself hereafter
when body and soul are no longer together?

MARCH

The pupil learns whatever the master has mastered.
The science master can teach a keen student science.
A theologian can impart theology,
and a grammarian grammar.
All these forms of knowledge can help you in life,
but at death only knowledge of emptiness
will be your rations to sustain you on the road.

MARCH

The intellectual quest is exquisite like pearls and coral,
but it is not the same as the spiritual quest.
The spiritual quest is on another level altogether.
Spiritual wine has a subtler taste.
The intellect and the senses investigate cause and effect.
The spiritual seeker surrenders to wonder.

20
MARCH

Gnosis is experiencing the fire directly,
not prattling on about smoke.
All this pompous noise
about spiritual "authority"
is only a way of saying to the world,
"I can't see anything. Please excuse me."

21
MARCH

The book of Sufi wisdom
is not written on the blank page,
but on a heart white as virgin snow.
Scholars pursue penmarks.
Sufis track footprints in the snow,
like hunters tracing a musk-deer's trail,
until they breathe in the sweet scent
that the deer exudes from its navel,
and rush to catch their quarry.

22
MARCH

Your glorification of God
is just an exhalation from clay and water.
It only becomes a bird of paradise
when your heart breathes sincerity into it.

23

MARCH

Stop speaking and let Spirit speak through you.

24

MARCH

The fake teacher is like a professional mourner
whose only motive is money.
The professional mourner utters words of burning grief,
but his heart is not even warm.

25

MARCH

The tongue is a curtain covering the soul.
When the wind blows we get to see what's inside the house.
Pearls and grains of wheat perhaps?
Or maybe snakes and scorpions?
Or a treasure guarded by a serpent,
since gold is never left without a guardian?

26
MARCH

Listen, tongue, you are an unspendable treasure.
Listen, tongue, you are a disease without cure.

27
MARCH

Make a habit of shutting up.

28
MARCH

If you're not a tongue of God then be an ear.

29

MARCH

A deaf man's neighbor was ill. He thought to himself:
"If I visit this poor young man, I will not be able to hear a
thing he says. But if I don't go, he will think I am heartless.
I will just have to guess what he is saying. First I will say:
'How are you feeling, my unfortunate friend.' He will then
reply: 'I am OK' or something like that. Then I will say:
'Thank God. What have you had to drink?' He will then reply,
'Some sherbet' or perhaps 'Some bean soup,'
and I will say, 'Excellent! What doctor is looking after you?'
He will then reply, 'Dr. So-and-so,' and I will say, 'That's good.
You are very lucky to be in such safe hands.'"
Having prepared carefully, the deaf man made his visit.
"How are you?" he asked.
"Dying," replied the sick man faintly.
"Thank God," said the deaf man,
"What have you had to drink?"
"Poison," whispered the sick man.
"Excellent! Which doctor is looking after you?"
asked the deaf man.
"The angel of Death," spluttered the sick man, turning pale.
"That's good. You are very lucky to be in such safe hands,"
said the deaf man,
and he left feeling very pleased with himself.
The invalid, on the other hand, was left wondering what he
had ever done to make his neighbor hate him so much.

30

MARCH

Wisdom repeated like a parrot
flies away when you most need it.
I'm telling you, Mr Clever-Clever,
even if you write it down in your little book
and brag about how well-read you are,
it will escape from this cage.
Forget about what other people have said.
Just show Wisdom some love and affection,
and She will become a pet bird
whose perch is your open palm.

31

MARCH

Your intellect wants to fly upward,
but your conventional ideas
keep you feeding below in the bird tray.

1

APRIL

Conventional wisdom is borrowed,
second-hand opinion
that we pass off as our own.
Enough of this common nonsense!

2

APRIL

A fool who was walking with Jesus saw some bones in a
ditch and begged him, "Teach me the secret Name with the
power to raise the dead so that I can bring
this poor wretch back to life."
Jesus replied, "It is not your place to use the Name.
It requires a deeper understanding."
"If I'm not up to it, then you do it," insisted the fool.
And he went on and on like this until reluctantly Jesus spoke
the Name over the bones. Immediately he did so, the bones
became clothed with flesh and were transformed into a wild
lion which tore open the fool's skull. But, as you might
imagine, there was nothing inside.

3

APRIL

Hey, Mr Scientist!
How will it help you to know about everything
in the universe,
if you don't know anything about yourself?

4

APRIL

When you say to a thirsty man,
"Over here! There's water in this cup,"
does the thirsty man reply,
"That is only your opinion.
Where is the evidence
to substantiate your assertion
that this is an aqueous liquid?"

5
APRIL

When a mother cries to her suckling babe,
"Come to me child. I am your mother,"
Does the child answer, "So you claim.
Show me some proof.
Then I will comfort myself
feeding at your breast."

6
APRIL

Some Indians kept an elephant in a dark room.
As it was impossible to see the elephant, those who
wanted to know something about this exotic beast had to feel
it with their hands. The first person went into the darkness
and felt the elephant's trunk and announced,
"This creature is like a water pipe."
The next person felt the elephant's ear and asserted,
"No. It's like a giant fan."
A third person felt the elephant's leg and declared,
"That's not true. This animal resembles a pillar."
A fourth person felt the elephant's back and concluded,
"Not at all. It's like a throne."
Different points of view produce different opinions.
If someone had brought in a candle, they would've
all felt like fools.

7
APRIL

Don't just guess which is fool's gold
and which is the real thing.

If you don't have your own touchstone,
make friends with someone who does.

8
APRIL

Wherever you go traveling
always search for the Keeper of the Treasure.

9
APRIL

A man gave some money to four friends – a Persian,
an Arab, a Turk, and a Greek. The Persian suggested,
"Let's spend this on angur."
"No," said the Arab, "I want to spend the money on inab."
The Turk demanded, "We should spend the money on uzum."
The Greek shouted, "Stop all this arguing.
We're going to buy istafil."
And so they began to fight – all because they did not know
that each one of them was talking about grapes.

10
APRIL

Galen once asked one of his companions for a particular
medicine for madness. The companion replied, "Master,
you're a great scientist; why do you need this medicine?"
Galen replied, "Just then, a madman looked at me like an old
friend, pulled my sleeve and winked at me. If there had not
been some bond of similarity between us, how could this man
have been so familiar? People only feel that way toward one
of their own kind."

This is true. When two people touch each other deeply, there
is undoubtedly something in common between them. Birds
fly only with their own flock. The only place we are familiar
with those with whom we have no affinity is in the grave.

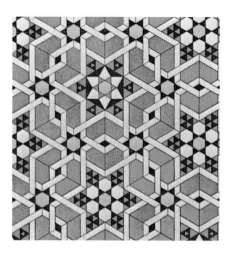

11
APRIL

A greengrocer had a parrot which was excellent at talking.
It was famous for sitting outside the shop and exchanging
pleasantries with customers. One day, the parrot flew off its
perch and spilled an expensive bottle of rose oil.
When the owner saw what had happened, he was furious, and
struck the bird on the head so hard that its feathers fell out,
leaving it bald-headed. The parrot was so shocked that it
never spoke again. The grocer was heartbroken and full of
remorse. He begged every passing Sufi to persuade the parrot
to speak again, but nothing would work. That is, until one day
a bald-headed Master came into the shop, and the parrot
looked up and remarked, "What! Did you spill a bottle of
rose oil as well?" Everyone in the shop laughed, but how
many of us also project onto others our experience and so
completely misunderstand the truth?

APRIL

The parrot focuses on its reflection,
believing that the parrot in the mirror
is teaching it how to speak.
Actually the Master is hiding behind the mirror.
The parrot learns easily
because it is fooled into thinking
it is learning from one of its own kind.
It has no idea about the old fox
who is really doing the talking.
Although it has learned everything from a man,
the parrot still has no notion
of what it is like to be a human being.

In the same way,
an egotistical student presumes
that his Master is the same as he is.
He doesn't see Universal Consciousness
hiding behind the mirror,
teaching him through the man
that he believes to be speaking.
He learns the words spoken,
but knows nothing of the true speaker.
How can he?
He is still only a parrot,
not a companion on the Way.

APRIL

Abú Jahl saw Muhammad and said:
"What an ugly son of a bitch!"
Muhammad replied:
"You're rude, but you're right."
Abú Bakr saw Muhammad and said:
"You're the beautiful shining sun!"
Muhammad said:
"You're right, my friend.
You've seen through."
Someone listening to this asked:
"How can they both be right
when they are contradicting each other?"
Muhammad said:
"I am a mirror polished by Allah.
In me everyone sees themselves."

APRIL

The lover of this world
is admiring a wall which the sunbeams strike.

He is like a drowning man
clinging for safety to someone else who can't swim.

15

APRIL

Appearances are husks —
the seed is hidden.

16

APRIL

Make it a habit to look at the Light directly,
not from indoors through a window,
so that, when the window inevitably shatters,
you aren't blinded.

17

APRIL

The heart is not a wall reflecting moonbeams
of Divine Light.
To the Gnostic, it is a door which opens onto Reality.

18

APRIL

While you're drunk senseless on sensation,
you won't even notice the cup of mystical intoxication.

19

APRIL

All these homes were once architect's fantasies.
Those substantial walls were brought into being by ideas.
Everything starts as someone's dream.
Take a fresh look at the world around you.
Isn't it all ideas in action?
First the thought, then the realization.
That's how the temporally manifest
emerges from eternal potentiality.

20

APRIL

Consciousness is a king.
Ideas are his envoys.

21
APRIL

The bird is soaring sky-high,
but its shadow flies on the ground.
You are chasing the shadow,
oblivious to the fact that the shadow
is a fleeting image of the bird.
It doesn't matter if you empty
a belt full of bullets upon it;
you won't catch your quarry.

22
APRIL

Everyone is infatuated by some crazy fantasy
of what will make them fulfilled and happy.
One person wants to be stinking rich
and so works through the night selling stocks and shares,
or risks his life as a mercenary in someone else's war.
Another person trades his lifetime for regular money
and a nine-to-five job with few surprises.
Someone else becomes religious,
spending his days being "holy" and otherworldly.
Everyone looks at everyone else and says to themselves,
"Why on earth are they wasting their lives doing that?"

23
APRIL

Until you've grown your own beard,
don't ridicule smooth chins.

24
APRIL

Stop squatting in this briny puddle of a self.
Buy a big Self that courses like a freshwater river.

25
APRIL

A thirsty man was standing on a high wall near a river.
He wanted water as if he were a fish on dry land,
but the height of the wall prevented him from reaching the river.
He tore a brick from the wall and threw it into the water.
The splash was like the sweetest word
he had ever heard from a well-loved friend.
The sound intoxicated him like wine,
so he tore up other bricks and threw them in also.
"Hey, you – Mr Brick-Thrower!" called the water.
"Why are you pelting me with bricks?"
"For two reasons," replied the thirsty man.
"First, just to hear the sweet sound of 'plop.'
Second, because, with every brick I throw,
the wall becomes lower and I get closer to the water."

26

APRIL

The thirsty scour the world for water,
but water is also searching for the thirsty.

27

APRIL

You want water?!
What are you talking about?
You are up to your knees in a river!

28

APRIL

"**C**ome on in," said the water to the dirty man.
"I'm embarrassed to be so dirty.
I'll make you muddy," replied the man.
"But if you don't come in,
you'll never stop being ashamed," said the water.

29

APRIL

Clean the heart-mirror
so that you can distinguish
ugliness from beauty.

30

APRIL

A human being is a jungle.
Be wary if you are from the Divine Breath.
There are hundreds and thousands of wolves
and wild hogs in there waiting.
This forest is full of ghouls and fairies.

1
MAY

If you pause for a moment from feeding your face,
you're immediately off trying to get laid.
You still wouldn't be happy even if
you owned a chain of restaurants and whorehouses.

You started off as a snake –
now you've become a seven-headed dragon.
The trap is baited with greed. Stop biting!

2
MAY

That big black serpent was once a worm.
Eventually it became a dragon.
But in the hands of Moses,
Allah turned it into a walking stick.

3
MAY

Grab your donkey by the neck
and point him where you are going.
Let him wander for a moment
and he'll have his head down in hay.
Be warned!
He's an old enemy of the Way,
this friend of fodder.

4
MAY

If some cunning thief steals all your wealth,
a robber will have stolen a robber.

5

MAY

A little mouse caught a camel's tether in its paws by
accident. Wherever he went, the camel followed him, and the
mouse soon became puffed up with pride, believing
himself to be its master.

The camel, however, planned to teach this little impostor a
lesson. After some time, the mouse stopped
at the edge of a large river.

"Why are you hesitating?" asked the camel. "Walk
out into the water. You are a great leader."

"This is a very big river," replied the little
mouse. "I'm frightened of being drowned."

"It is only up to my shins," said the camel.
"What are you worried about?"

"To you, it is an ant, but to me, it is a dragon,"
said the dismayed mouse.

"Well, don't be so arrogant next time, Mr Mouse,"
said the camel. "Now, jump up onto my hump and I'll
take you over this little stream."

6
M A Y

A man asked a tattoo artist, "Please tattoo me with a raging
lion to show the world how courageous I am."
But when the needles started to prick him, the man began
squealing, "Stop! You're killing me. What are you doing?"
The tattoo artist replied, "I am tattooing
a lion, just as you asked."
"Which bit are you tattooing?" asked the man.
"The tail," replied the artist.
"Well, this lion doesn't need a tail.
Forget it and go on," said the man.
The artist began to work again, but the man began
howling, "Now what are you doing?"
"I am tattooing the lion's ears," replied the artist.
"Well, let's do without ears as well," said the man.
But, as soon as the artist began to use his needle once more,
the man started shrieking, "What now?"
"I am tattooing the lion's belly," replied the artist.
"Then leave out the belly. The lion will be fine without it,"
yelled the man. At this, the tattoo artist threw down the
needle in disgust and announced, "Whoever saw a lion
with no tail, ears or belly. This lion will only tell the
world what a coward you are."

7
M A Y

Small heroes subdue their enemies.
Big heroes conquer themselves.

8
M A Y

How long are you going to go on planning
to conquer the world and fill it full of yourself?

9
M A Y

When selfishness comes, goodness goes.

10
M A Y

Don't lock your door when the enemy is in the house.

 11

MAY

Many of the faults you see in others
are your own faults reflected back to you.
Actually you are branding and blaming yourself.

 12

MAY

The fault is in the blamer.
Spirit sees nothing to criticize.

 13

MAY

Friends become enemies
because we see them as separate from us.
But in reality, we are quarreling with ourselves.

 14

MAY

Even if you don't have the same fault as
someone you are criticizing, perhaps
you will develop that fault later in your life.
Think about that!

 15

MAY

All the saints and sages say
that evil deeds become a dark well
which enclose the evil-doer.
The worse the doer's deed,
the darker is his well.
You may intend to snare someone else,
but you're digging that pit
for yourself to fall down.
Watch out! Don't dig too deep.

MAY

The world is a mountain
and our acts are shouts
which echo back to us.

MAY

Life lays different forms of fodder before us
to see what sort of animal we are.
When a wolf mates with an antelope
and you want to know the nature of their offspring,
drop bones and grass in front of it
and watch what happens.

MAY

Be soft earth,
so that you may sprout flowers of many colors.
You've been a jagged rock for years.
Just once – as an experiment – be earth!

MAY

Visit the sick, and you will heal yourself.
The ill person may be a Sufi Master,
and your kindness will be repaid in wisdom.
Even if the sick person is your enemy,
you will still benefit,
for kindness has the power to transform
sworn enemies into firm friends.
And if there is no healing of bad feeling,
there certainly will be less ill will,
because kindness is the greatest of all balms.

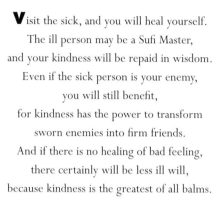

20

MAY

Adult conflicts are as meaningless as children's squabbles.

21

MAY

Be a slave not a king.
Be a ball not a bat.

22

MAY

Your flatterers will mock you,
once you are no longer
elegant and beautiful.
When you come to the door,
they will jeer, "Look out!
Here comes the living dead!"

23

MAY

If you gave it all away,
do you think God would be stingy?
When you sow seeds the barn is left empty,
but the ground is made rich.
If you leave the seeds in the barn,
all you'll have is a decaying feast
for the mice and weevils.

24

MAY

What are you talking about!
Having to earn a living
doesn't stop you digging for the Treasure.
Don't abandon your everyday life.
That's where the Treasure is hidden.

25

MAY

God says that, compared to the cash
you can earn in the spiritual world,
the currency of this world is Toy Town money.
You've set up shop here, but it's only pretense.
When the evening comes, you go home hungry to mommy.
The other children are gone and you are alone.
This world is a playground and death is the night.
Are you returning home, hungry and tired,
with a purse full of nothing but colored paper?

26

MAY

If thorns keep sucking up the water of your consciousness,
how are you ever going to grow ripe fruit?

27

MAY

Pay your debts early,
while you are still strong and robust.
While the spring of youth is ripening the fruit.
While the fountain of desire is overflowing with fertility.
While the house has its roof on straight
and the walls don't need buttresses.
Before the soil turns crumbly and barren.
Before your eyes grow dim and sunken
and your face looks like an old lizard.
For those who wait the day is late.
The donkey's lame and the way is long.
The shop is pilfered and the business is bankrupt.
The roots of bad habits are firmly embedded
and no power remains to wrench them out.

28

MAY

Don't beg for a crust from me
when you're carrying
a basket full of bread
on top of your head!

29

MAY

Are you just going to admire the jug
or are you actually going to drink the water?

30

MAY

I'm not weaving some exotic yarn.
Allah forbid!
This is hard cash,
here and now in your hand.
This is the way it is for you and me.
Think about it.

31

MAY

Watch out! Don't keep saying "tomorrow."
Many tomorrows have been and gone.
If you are not careful,
the time for planting will have passed.

SUMMER

SMEAR YOUR HANDS
WITH HIS HONEY

Summer is the time for celebration. God is waiting for you to smear your hands with His honey. He's been playing a game of hide-and-seek, but here's a clue – His home is your heart. Unlock the heart-door. You are pregnant with God. Give birth to your love-child. Let sweet love wash you clean of bitterness. Get drunk on devotion until you don't know what's what. Give up being so sensible; it's getting you nowhere. Try being spontaneous. Try a little madness. Strip off the concepts that clothe your consciousness and become aware of naked awareness. That's the doorway into the Presence. You'll know when you find what you're looking for, because it will taste so good. You won't need a certificate as proof. There will be no doubt. Are you ready to get your hands all sweet and sticky? Then catch the moment. That's not difficult. There is only this moment.

JUNE

God says, "I want you to delight in knowing Me.
I want you to smear your hands with My honey."

JUNE

The pay packet of the spiritual worker
bulges with rapture and ecstatic love.

JUNE

Love and imagination are magicians
who create an image of the Beloved in your mind
with which you share your secret intimate moments.

This apparition is made of nothing at all,
but from its mouth comes the question,
"Am I not your Loved One?"
and from you the soft reply "Yes. Yes. Yes."

JUNE

Allah says,
"You can't cram me into a jar.
Heaven and Earth
are too cramped to contain me.
I live only in the loving
expanses of a lover's heart.
Look for me there."

5

JUNE

It doesn't matter whether your loving is spiritual or sensual.
What matters is that it leads you to LOVE itself.

 6

JUNE

Love is unconditional kindness.

 7

JUNE

Those with loving hearts have helping hands.

 8

JUNE

Put a lid on the kettle and fill yourself
with love's boiling water!

 9

JUNE

When love consumes your heart
you always feel young.

 10

JUNE

Only Love makes agreements out of arguments.

 11

JUNE

Be amiable with everyone.
Like a maker of idols,
carve a friend out of the stone.

 12

JUNE

When you have cut this envelope of skin
into a lattice to let in spiritual light,
you can see a friend even with your eyes shut.

13

JUNE

Always be aware when someone is kind to you,
because you may discover the source of kindness.

14

JUNE

Mutual understanding arises
from speaking the same wisdom,
not speaking the same language.
Better to share one heart than one tongue.

15

JUNE

Love makes bitter things sweet.
Love turns copper to gold.

With love dregs settle into clarity.
With love suffering ceases.

Love brings the dead back to life.
Love transforms the king into a slave.

Love is the consummation of Gnosis.
How could a fool sit on such a throne?

JUNE

Love is pregnant with generations of lovers.

JUNE

A wise man is a wise man
because of the love in his heart,
not because of his white beard.

JUNE

The heart is pregnant with God,
and the Prophets are midwives.

JUNE

We witness many wonders when asleep.
In sleep the heart is turned into a window.
The Gnostics dream beautiful dreams while awake.
Suck into your eyes the dust from their feet.

20

JUNE

Bayazid was traveling on a pilgrimage to the Ka'aba in
Mecca when he met a crazy old man who asked him,
"What strange land are you lugging this baggage
of a body toward, Bayazid?"
Bayazid replied, "I'm off to the Ka'aba at dawn."
"Really," said the old man without much interest,
"And what provisions are you taking with you?"
"Two hundred silver coins sewn into my cloak,"
replied Bayazid.

The old man said, "Forget all that. It would do
you more good to give me the money, and then walk
around me seven times instead of the Ka'aba.
If you did that, you'd have achieved your real desire
and made the great pilgrimage.
You would awaken to eternal life.
By the truth of the Truth,
I tell you, Allah prefers me to the Ka'aba.
The Ka'aba may be his holiday home for religious occasions,
but my innermost consciousness is his permanent residence.
When you see me, you see Allah.
Be careful not to be confused by appearances.
Allah is not separate from me."

Bayazid put these words in his ears like golden earrings. From
this crazy old man, Bayazid learned to become a Master.

21

JUNE

When one bright intellect
meets another bright intellect,
the light increases
and the Way becomes clear.

22

JUNE

When one Master meets another,
the One meets the One.

23

JUNE

The inner consciousness
of the saint
is the true mosque
where all should worship.
God lives there.

24

JUNE

The Masters see more in a brick than you do in a mirror.
They were bathing in the Divine Bounty
before this world existed.

They lived for lifetimes before bodies were born.
They saw the harvest while the wheat was still seed.

They understood the meaning when it was unformulated.
They found the pearl although there wasn't an ocean.

25

JUNE

In Summer the Masters feel December frosts.
In sunbeams they detect shadows.
In grapes, they taste the wine.
In emptiness, they find everything they are looking for.

26

JUNE

When Mount Sinai saw Moses' radiant face,
it began to dance and became a perfect Sufi.
That's amazing when you think that a face is just flesh.

27

JUNE

Take a look at those flashy fakers
in their expensive designer clothing.
Does wearing a particular label
increase their understanding of life and death?
Does it quiet the scorpion of grief
that inhabits their heart?
On the outside they look dressed to kill,
but on the inside they are dying.

Now look over there at that old bum dressed in rags.
His thoughts are sharper than an Armani suit
and his words more exquisite than haute couture.

28

JUNE

One night, a Police Inspector found a drunk lying
at the bottom of a wall. "Hey you!" he called,
"What have you been drinking?"
"I have drunk what was in that jar," replied the drunk.
"Obviously," continued the Police Inspector,
"But what was inside the jar?"
"What I have drunk was inside the jar," insisted the drunk.
"Unfortunately that is now hidden inside you," complained
the Police Officer, exasperated by the vicious circle he found
himself circumambulating. Feeling like a donkey trying to get
itself out of the mud, he demanded, "Well, let's take a look,
shall we? Open up your mouth. Come on now, say 'Ahhhhh!'"
The drunk immediately laughed, "Ha! Ha! Ha!"
"I told you to say 'Ah!' What's all this 'Ha!' business?"
yelled the Inspector.
"'Ah!' describes suffering and grief. 'Ha!' is the inebriate's
expression of joy," explained the drunk.
"What are you going on about now? Don't try selling me any
mystical nonsense or tying me up in esoteric arguments –
just move along," ordered the Inspector.
"Get lost yourself. I'm not selling anything. If I were still
imprisoned in some sort of understanding of this unreal
existence of ours, I would be standing in the pulpit with the
professional priests doling out platitudes," said the drunk.
"That's it!," said the Inspector, "You're drunk and you're
coming with me to prison."

"My dear Inspector," slurred the drunk, "would you take the
shirt off a naked man's back? If I could have walked home,
I would have done so hours ago. And then this delightful
conversation we are sharing would never have happened."

 29

JUNE

The drunk sways home from the bar,
tottering this way and that,
and the children point and giggle.
Then into the mud he plunges.
And dancing at his heels
his infant disciples dissolve into laughter,
unaware of his inebriation or the taste of wine.
Let me tell you – you're still a kid,
until you've been stoned on God.

 30

JUNE

Spirituality is bewildering!
Not the mystification
caused by having your back to God.
But the mystery of ecstasy –
of drowning in God –
of being drunk with the Beloved.

JULY

Run away from good luck.
Drink poison and spit out water.
Insult anyone who praises you.
Lend your money to the destitute.
Stop looking for security
and start living dangerously.
Give up your good reputation
and cultivate some notoriety.
You've tried being sensible
and it's gotten you nowhere.
Try being crazy for a change.

JULY

Those who pretend to be sane
in such a mad world
are irredeemably deranged.

3

JULY

You won't win the Beloved's heart
except by losing your head.

4

JULY

Thinking is a friend who will help
you work out what to say and do,
but when it comes to ecstasy
he gets all confused.

5

JULY

Bewilderment is your entrance ticket
into the Mystery of the Presence.

6

JULY

Sell your cleverness and buy bewilderment.

7

JULY

Conventional knowledge advertizes itself
as a convenience product you can buy straight off the shelf.
Mystical knowledge doesn't come in such a fancy box,
and costs a lot more. But those who buy
close their lips and become enraptured by the trading.

8

JULY

It is wise to carefully discriminate
between the stronger of two alternative opinions,
but don't doubt that the sun is shining
when you can feel its warmth on your back.

9
JULY

You can tell what's true from what's false,
because the false makes you feel uneasy in your guts,
whereas the Truth fills your heart with quiet happiness.

10
JULY

An immediate intuitive apprehension of Truth
leaves no room for interpretation.

11
JULY

The bird of opinion has only one wing.
It jumps a few feet forward then falls to the ground.
And so it stumbles on, in hope of reaching its nest.
But when Knowledge gives that crippled bird
a second wing, it takes to the air like Gabriel,
leaving behind arguments and theories.
If everyone in the world were to say,
"You are on the Way to God,"
that bird would not feel more certain.
Or if all the world said, "You're on the wrong path.
You think you're a mountain,
but actually you're a blade of grass,"
heavy doubts would not ground that bird.
Even if the seas and mountains themselves
started shouting, "You're on the road to Hell,"
it would keep flying, because that bird is free.

12

JULY

There is a bird whose song thrills those who can hear it,
which flies forever from Allah to the Earth, and back again.

In comparison, any other bird is a bat.

13

JULY

Angels can't live on the earth.
Animals can't live in the heavens.

You have the body of an animal
and the spirit of an angel.

You can walk on the earth
and also soar in the heavens.

14

JULY

This world is a tree
and we are its ripening fruits.
Unripe fruits cling to the branches.
As they mature and become sweet,
they hold on less tightly.

15

JULY

The unripe can't understand what it feels like to be ready.

17

JULY

To the fool,
every aspect of the world is a fetter.

To the wise,
every situation is an opportunity to break free.

18

JULY

Close your ears and then listen.
Still your mind and then be mindful.

19

JULY

Life is arriving fresh in each instant,
but has the semblance of continuity –
like water when it's flowing fast
appears to be a permanent river,
like a sparkler when you whirl it around your head
appears to be a continuous circle of light.

16

JULY

From this flapping piece of flesh called "tongue,"
teachings are flowing like a flood
into that emptiness called "ears"
to inundate the orchard of consciousness
and ripen the fruit of wisdom.

20

JULY

The Gnostics have an eye ointment
which can correct faulty vision.

While you watch the river of time,
they are aware of the Ocean of Always.

21

JULY

Muhammad said, "The world is this moment."

22

JULY

How can I know anything about the past or the future,
when the light of the Beloved shines only NOW.

23

JULY

The Sufi is the child of NOW.
No one on the Way says "tomorrow."

24

JULY

Past and future are shutters
covering the window
through which streams
God's sunlight.

25

JULY

The house may be full of light,
but only the sun is light-giving.

26

JULY

"**I** am luminous. This is my light," brags the old wall.
"Oh yeah?," says the sun,
"Well, let's see what happens when I set!"
"We have grown green all by ourselves,"
boast the young plants.
"Oh yeah?," says the Summer,
"Tell me that when Autumn comes!"
"I am so beautiful," admires the body.
"Don't give me that, you dunghill," says Spirit,
"I have shone my light on you,
and you have come to life for a few short days.

27

JULY

Wine becomes drunk on the drinker,
not the drinker on the wine.

The body came into being from consciousness,
not consciousness from the body.

We are bees and we have made the body,
cell by cell, like a honeycomb.

28

JULY

You're looking at the waves but ignoring the Sea.

29
JULY

One part of the Whole is not separate from the other parts.
The beauty of all flowers is part of the rose's beauty.
The coo of the turtledove is part of the nightingale's song.

30
JULY

The delight of the part lies in appreciating the Whole.

31
JULY

God says,
"Don't you think My sky is awesome and beautiful?
Why don't you pay it more attention?
Don't be content with a quick glance.
Look again and again.
Then tell me – does it have a single flaw?"

1
AUGUST

Let me stop looking at myself and start looking at You,
for you are nearer to me than I am to myself.

2
AUGUST

One day Moses came across a humble old shepherd in the
desert, who was privately talking to Allah. The shepherd's
tone was relaxed and familiar. He told Allah how he wanted
to help Him, to pick the lice off of Him, to wash His clothes,
to kiss His feet and hands. He ended his prayer with,
"When I think of You, all I can say is 'Ahhhhh!'"
Moses was appalled and exclaimed, "Do you realize that you
are talking to the Creator of Heaven and Earth,
not to your old uncle?!"
The shepherd felt very foolish and asked Moses if he thought
Allah would ever forgive him. However, as the shepherd
began to sadly wander off into the desert to repent, a divine
voice spoke to Moses, rebuking him.

"Moses, what to you seems wrong is right to him.
One man's poison is another man's honey.
Purity and impurity, sloth and diligence –
what do these matter to me?
I am above all that.
Ways of worship can't be ranked as better or worse,
It is all praise and it is all right.
It is the worshiper who is glorified by worship – not I.
I don't listen to the words.
I look inside at the humility.
Only that low and open emptiness is real.
Forget language – I want burning! Burning!
Be friends with this fire.
Burn up your grand ideas and special words!"

3
AUGUST

A prayer is a prayer only when it's prayed in the Presence.

4
AUGUST

All night, a man called "Allah" –
until his lips were bleeding.
Then the Devil said, "Hey! Mr Gullible!
How come you've been calling all night
and never once heard Allah say, 'Here I am'?
You call out so earnestly and, in reply, what?
I'll tell you what. Nothing!"
The man suddenly felt empty and abandoned.
Depressed, he threw himself on the ground
and fell into a deep sleep.
In a dream, he met Abraham, who asked,
"Why are you regretting praising Allah?"
The man said, "I called and called
but Allah never replied 'Here I am.'"
Abraham explained, "Allah has said,
'Your calling My Name is My reply.
Your longing for Me is My message to you.
All your attempts to reach Me
are in reality My attempts to reach you.
Your fear and love are a noose to catch Me.
In the silence surrounding every call of 'Allah'
waits a thousand replies of 'Here I am.'"

5
AUGUST

The Artist is hiding in His studio.
Go in and sneak a peek.
The weave of His work conceals the Creator.
From outside His workshop,
you'd never know He even exists.
But step out of the painting
and you will understand
the portrait and the Painter.
Only nude models are allowed in this studio.
Everyone outside is forced to wear a blindfold.

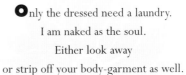

6
AUGUST

A man went to the rose garden
in search of beautiful blooms,
but found the beauty he craved
in the face of the gardener.

7
AUGUST

I came to Your court
in search of wealth,
but when I entered the hall
I became Your throne.

8
AUGUST

Only the dressed need a laundry.
I am naked as the soul.
Either look away
or strip off your body-garment as well.

Is it too much to go completely nude?
Well at least wear less
to cover up what you really are.

9
AUGUST

I am burning with Love of God.
Does anyone need a light?

You can set your rubbish ablaze
from the fire within me.

10
AUGUST

In this fire, I have seen a world
in which every atom breathes
with the spirit-breath of Jesus.
That world appears non-existent
but is the essence of existence.
This world appears substantial,
but actually is impermanent.

11
AUGUST

Does the world seem like a big place?
Well, to Omnipresence, it's atomic.

12
AUGUST

You could easily presume I am sleeping.
My eyes are closed, but my heart is wide awake.

Do I seem as if I'm doing nothing?
That's not such an easy thing to do!

Muhammad said, "My eyes sleep,
but my heart is awake to my Creator."

Your eyes are alert, but your heart is snoring.
Mine are locked, but my heart gives free access.

13
AUGUST

I've sold myself to God for hard cash.
All those other customers were bankrupts.
Their funny money is no good to me!

14

AUGUST

This is great!
I've turned into a plantation of sugarcane.
Sweetness is growing inside me
and at the same time I get to eat it!

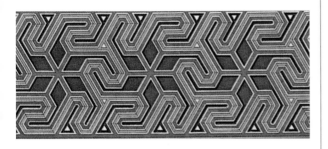

15

AUGUST

Help me, Doctor! I'm gone again.
Beloved! I'm raving and frenzied.
Each link in Your time-chain is unique and multileveled,
so I suffer a new sort of madness in each moment.

16

AUGUST

I have been wasting away –
ever since I learned the secret mysteries
of eternal life through dying to self.

17

AUGUST

This pining for Your love
has knocked me senseless so many times,
I'm punch drunk.

18

AUGUST

Dam the torrent of ecstasy
before it floods,
or be engulfed in devastation!

What do I care about that?
Under the wreckage is buried Treasure.

19

AUGUST

I am a shadow in love with the sun.
When You rise I set.

20

AUGUST

If I had any idea of what I'm doing,
do you think I'd be so mad with melancholy
and ranting nonsensically like this?
My brain is empty,
so don't blame this raving on me!
It's His fault.
He robbed me of my reason.
In His Presence rationality is anesthetized.

21
AUGUST

When mouthfuls of food
turn to pearls inside you,
don't hold back! Eat up!
Eat as much as you can!

22
AUGUST

Hey! Comrade-of-the-Heart!
Forget how tired you are for a second
and listen to me sing a love song to Beauty.
Watch me paint a reflection
of the Beloved's complexion.
Just trying to talk about it
makes me feel my body's going to burst.
I'm like a happy ant in a big granary,
dragging away a little grain,
which is just too much for me to bear.

23
AUGUST

The Arab word for "Spirit" is feminine.
So what? Where's the harm in that!
Spirit has nothing to do with male or female.
How could Spirit be dry or moist?
It doesn't grow fat from eating bread.
It doesn't suffer from mood swings.

24
AUGUST

So I dare to call Allah my "Lover"!
Don't blame me!
I'd shut up from fear of offending,
if He would just let up on me for a moment.
But He keeps on encouraging me,
enthusing, "Rave on!
There's nothing wrong in it.
It's your divine destiny."

25

AUGUST

I confess.
I am an obsessive.
But my obsession
liberates me into Love.
Your obsession
confines you in a prison.

26

AUGUST

The rose and the nightingale can't speak –
but just listen to what passes between them!

Listen to what the candle is saying to the moth.
You can't translate that into words!

27

AUGUST

If the seven seas turned to ink,
my pen would still run dry.

If every orchard was cut into pencils,
I'd wear them all away.

The Word cannot be expressed in words.

28
AUGUST

It doesn't matter what I say about Love;
when Love arrives I feel ashamed of myself.

My wagging tongue is a great clarifier,
but Love is too clear to be clarified.

My pen was absorbed in writing,
but split in two when it wrote "LOVE."

My intellect became like an old donkey
unable to pull itself out of the mud.

Only Love elucidates Love.

29
AUGUST

I was making up poems when my Sweetheart said,
"Why are you thinking of anything but Me?
Relax, my troubled troubadour —
in My presence, you are already rhymed with happiness.
Why are you bothering with words?
Don't mix thorns with the fruit.
I will whirl you around
until words and thoughts are so confused
that you can talk My language."

30
AUGUST

What is love?
You will never know
until you lose yourself
in the Beloved.

31
AUGUST

The lover is afraid that if he speaks
the pearl may fall out of his mouth.

FALL

THE REED PIPE HOWLS
ABOUT SEPARATION

Fall is the time of passing light. Clouds crowd out the sun. The drunk wakes sober again, but with a hangover. The beating drum of the dance is replaced by the lamenting pipe. Honey has turned to vinegar. Did you think you'd arrived? You have hardly begun. Writing love letters is just a sign of separation. Don't pretend to be wise; you'll only make a fool of yourself. Howl with grief. It will make you real. You feel abandoned because, whenever you arrive, the Beloved leaves. Was it something you said? Yes. You said you wanted Oneness. So now the Beloved never shows up when you are around. It's you or Him. Make your choice. The Beloved is waiting for "you" to drown in His sea of selflessness.

1

SEPTEMBER

Hear how the reed pipe
howls about separation.
"Since being ripped
from the river bed,
I have sung dirges —
yearning for another
torn-apart heart
who understands
my lament of longing.
Everyone abandoned
far from home
craves reunion."

2

SEPTEMBER

Whose voice is it that echoes
in the mountains of my heart?
Sometimes I am resonant –
other times silent and empty.
Whoever You are – Master – Wise One –
fill these hills with Your reverberations once again.

3

SEPTEMBER

You are honey.
We are vinegar.

4

SEPTEMBER

Singing glory to You is not praise,
just proof of separation.

5

SEPTEMBER

I'm moaning.
That means I must be sober again.

Drunks are selfless and don't worry.

6

SEPTEMBER

It is better I don't talk.
The fire in my heart
is raging too fiercely.
The lion of separation
is frenzied and thirsty.

7

SEPTEMBER

What you want may be sweet as honey,
but what your Beloved wants is no desires.

8

SEPTEMBER

The seductive whisperings of desire
are the howls of a wolf that can tear a man to pieces.

9

SEPTEMBER

How long are you going to worry
about what has already happened and can't be changed,
and what has yet to come and can't be controlled?

You're all knotted up like an old reed,
unfit to share secrets with the flute player's lips.

 10

SEPTEMBER

Looking within is painful,
but it will split open the veil.

Until a mother goes into labor,
the child can't be born.

 11

SEPTEMBER

If a thorn in the foot is so damn difficult to find,
how much harder is it to find a thorn in the heart?
Answer me that!

 12

SEPTEMBER

If any Tom, Dick or Harry could find the thorn in the soul,
how would sorrow ever overcome anyone?
If you stick a thorn in a donkey's rump,
the donkey just bucks and has no idea how to get rid of it.
The more he struggles the deeper in it goes.
It needs someone smart to extract that thorn.

13
SEPTEMBER

God has been scaring the crap out of you
because, in His loving-kindness,
he wants to root you in real security.

14
SEPTEMBER

A bird is eating a worm when a cat pounces.
Devoured while devouring!
The preoccupied hunter forgets
he also is being hunted.
The plant drinks water for the animal
which will later digest it.
Only God devours nothing
and is devoured by nothing.
Everything else better look out!
Those who feel safe are really in danger.

You are fodder for your fantasies.
Desires are hornets and sleep is water
into which they plunge at night,
only to re-emerge each morning —
buzzing about inside you.
Chasing you this way and that.

15

SEPTEMBER

Testing times are a furnace
to extract silver from dross.

16

SEPTEMBER

You have to endure a lot of discomfort
while you are straining off the dregs.

17

SEPTEMBER

The world is whirling
because you are giddy.
It is you that is spinning –
not the world.

18

SEPTEMBER

How will you become a clear mirror
if you resent being polished?

19

SEPTEMBER

If you want to shine bright like the day,
burn up your dark night-self.

SEPTEMBER

We are imprisoned in this world,
until we confess to being bankrupts.

SEPTEMBER

Suffering is a giftbox
containing mercy.

Scrape off the rind.
The kernel is fresh.

SEPTEMBER

The ignorant moth desires the light but not the fire.
The mystic moth desires the fire to get to the Light.

SEPTEMBER

The thirsty man
who doesn't understand
that thunderclaps herald rain
complains that the booming
gives him a headache.

24

SEPTEMBER

Brother! To live in a dark cold house,
patiently putting up with pain and grief,
is actually life-enhancing.

The highs are hidden in the lows.
Spring is immanent in Autumn
and Autumn is fulfilled by Spring.
Don't run away from anything.

25

SEPTEMBER

God gave to Pharaoh so much wealth
that he imagined himself to be divine.
In his whole life he never had a spiritual headache,
so he never felt the need to moan to God.
God gave him the greatest empire in the world,
but he gave him no grief, pain or sorrow.
But grief is better than an empire
because it compels you to secretly call to God.

26

SEPTEMBER

The griefless call to God with a frozen heart.
But the call of the grief-stricken is saturated
with sincerity and authentic passion.

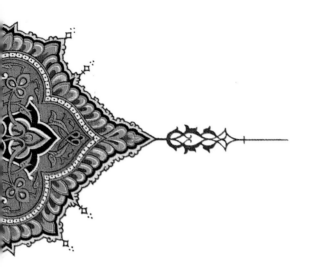

28

SEPTEMBER

Parched lips are a message from the water.

29

SEPTEMBER

Unlike all other sicknesses,
the lover's sickness is healthy.

30

SEPTEMBER

Originally we were all breathed
by the animating Spirit of Jesus.
But while we live in the body,
the in-breath is a wound
and the out-breath a bandage.
If the body-box were removed,
we would all be Christ.

27

SEPTEMBER

Medicine seeks pain.
Wherever suffering is,
the remedy goes there.

Water travels to lowlands.
If you want a drink of mercy,
become lowly and wait.
The Waters of Life will
rise up over your head like a flood.

OCTOBER

From one point of view, of course,
the parts are not connected to the Whole;
otherwise the Prophets would be out of a job!

OCTOBER

Lift up a broken hand in prayer.
Allah's perfect kindness is given away free
to all those who acknowledge their flaws.

3

OCTOBER

If you get stung by a wasp you can pull out the stinger,
but this invisible stinging is self-inflicted.
The violent pain continues unrelieved,
until you no longer have a self.
I keep wanting to warn you about this,
but worry it may make you depressed.

Ask for help from Him
who always comes when you call.
Say: "Forgive me, You who loves to forgive.
You are the cure for this gangrenous ME."

4

OCTOBER

You keep holding tight to "you" and "me."
Don't you see that these two obscure the One?

5

OCTOBER

You say that the part is connected to the Whole;
well, eat the thorns – they are connected to the rose.

6

OCTOBER

Let me paint a parable for you.
There is a river of fresh water
and a world-consuming fire.
Few desire fire. Most want water.
But some sort of topsy-turvy game is being played,
because those who immolate themselves in the flames
find themselves floating in cool water,
while those who bathe themselves in the water
re-emerge in the scorching flames.
Very few understand this Mystery,
so very few voluntarily choose fire.

7

OCTOBER

Listen, my heart,
as long as you feel any difference
between joy and sorrow,
you will be torn to pieces.

8

OCTOBER

When colorless Unity became a captive of color,
Moses and Pharaoh came into conflict.
When you regain your original neutrality,
Moses and Pharaoh will be at peace.
If you ask me about this mystery, I'll answer,
"Where there's color, clashes are unavoidable."

9

OCTOBER

Since God formed oil from water,
why do water and oil war with each other?

Since roses and thorns grow on the same plant,
why is one sharp and the other fragrant?

Or is this not really warfare?
Is it all part of the Divine Plan?

Is it more like bickering between donkey-traders?
Or is it neither of these? Is it just mystery?

The Treasure is hidden under this bewilderment.

10

OCTOBER

What does it matter
whether life is a calm lake
or a turbid torrent?
It doesn't last.
Millions of animals
live without worrying.
The dove doesn't know
if she'll eat tonight,
but she's singing anyway.
From elephant to gnat,
all are God's family
and rely on Him –
the Great Provider –
for nourishment.

OCTOBER

Since the beginning of your existence
the Transmuter has not abandoned you
to one permanent state of being,
but has evolved you
through a hundred thousand forms –
each one better than the last.
All change is a gift from the Transmuter.

OCTOBER

You have only been able to live many lives
because you have also suffered many deaths,
so why are you worried about dying?
Were any of those deaths really a loss?
Why are you clinging to this particular body?
Since each death has brought you a better life,
why not trust the Transmuter?

OCTOBER

Your fear of death is actually fear of confronting your Self.

OCTOBER

"**L**ife would be better if it didn't end in death."
What nonsense!
Without death life is meaningless.
It would be a harvest left to rot.

15

OCTOBER

Don't be frightened of non-existence.
It's in this world of more and less
that all the bills endlessly mount up.
Existence is expensive.
Non-existence is where we get paid.

16

OCTOBER

Look at yourself trembling with fear of non-existence.
Don't you realize that non-existence is constantly trembling
with fear that God will suddenly bring it into existence?

17

OCTOBER

The dead and buried
become trees
who lift up their arms
to call the deaf.
With their long fingers
and green tongues,
they divulge the secrets
of the Earth's heart.

18

OCTOBER

This world is a passing dream
which the sleeper is convinced is real,
until unexpectedly the dawn of death
frees him from this fantasy.

19

OCTOBER

What use is a fancy tomb
with grand domes
and high turrets
to a devotee of Reality?

20

OCTOBER

The mind sees things inside-out.
What it takes to be life is really death
and what it takes to be death is really life.

Allah, show us the way things really are.
Lead us through this hall of mirrors.

21

OCTOBER

A pretty girl ends up an ugly old donkey.
From angel to eyesore in a few years!
In human beings, beauty is only borrowed.
Bit by bit, God recalls the loan.
Day by day, the sapling withers.

Do you know the text which goes:
"Those who are given the gift of life
are also sentenced to decay?"
I've been thinking about that.
Now I'm looking for Beauty itself.
I've quit falling in love with bones.

22

OCTOBER

You can't see the Beloved,
so it's better to be blind.
Otherwise you may fall for a lover
who's here today and gone tomorrow.

23

OCTOBER

Form gets in the way of Reality.
When you are caught up in forms,
you are worshiping idols.

24

OCTOBER

The mother of all idols is the idol you call "ME."

25

OCTOBER

Don't burden your Spirit with your body's problems.
That's like getting Jesus to carry your pack
while your donkey is off frisking in the meadow.

26

OCTOBER

Dust blown by the wind.
Playing. Making a veil.
Feigning magic tricks.

These busy appearances
are really idle empty husks.
The seed is hidden.

Dust is a tool in the hands of the wind.
The eye of dust sees dust.
The eye that sees the wind
is another sort of eye altogether.

27

OCTOBER

Rub your eyes!
That's not an expensive necklace you are wearing.
That's the snake.

28

OCTOBER

A sage was riding along on his horse when he saw a snake
slip into the mouth of a sleeping man. It was too late to catch
the snake, so he hit the sleeper hard with a stick. This woke
him suddenly and sent him scampering for protection under a
tree. The sage picked up a number of fallen rotten apples and
stuffed them into the poor man's mouth.
"What are you doing to me?
What have I ever done to offend you?" cried the man.
As he began to curse angrily, the sage beat him with a stick,
shouting, "Run! Run into the wilderness!"
Sleepy, confused, stuffed with bad apples and forced to run
until he dropped, the poor man's stomach could no longer
take it. He vomited, and out shot the apples —
and among them the snake.
Seeing it writhing there, the man fell down in front of the
sage and thanked him over and over again.
"If I had told you about the snake," said the sage, "you would
have been frozen with fear and you wouldn't have had the
power to eat the rotten apples or vomit up the snake."

29

OCTOBER

A thief stole a man's pet snake. The snake bit the thief and he died. When the original owner saw the dead body of the thief, he remarked, "Well, look at that. My stolen snake robbed the thief of his life. I was begging God day and night that I might find this thief and get back my snake. Thank God my prayers went unheeded; otherwise, this could have been me. What I thought was a loss was actually a gain."

30

OCTOBER

One day, a nobleman ran up to Solomon, calling out, "Please help me, great sage. I have seen Azrael, the angel of Death, staring at me with a menacing look. Use your magic to transport me far from here to India where I will be safe." Solomon said "Okay. If that's really what you want," and he commanded the wind to carry the man to India.
The next day, Solomon asked Azrael, "What sort of menacing look did you give that poor man, to drive him from his home in such a hurry?"
Azrael replied, "I didn't give him a menacing look at all. In fact, I was looking at him because I was puzzled. God had commanded me to seize this man's soul while he was in India, but he was here in your palace, and I had no idea how I was going to obey God's wishes."

31

OCTOBER

It is the destiny of unbelievers not to believe in destiny.

1

NOVEMBER

Mind and body are under His control.
One moment He makes me a kernel.
The next He makes me rind.
When He wants me to be a cornfield,
I am suddenly green.
When He wants me to be ugly,
I find that I am decaying yellow.
Now I am a moon –
then the next minute it's all dark.
He's like that.

2

NOVEMBER

A devotee who regards himself
as the source of his devotion
is no stainless mirror.
He is a hunter who hasn't caught the bird.
Purge yourself of so-called "free will."
Know God to be the author of all actions.
Then you will be really free.

3

NOVEMBER

Take our hands and help us
to escape from our own hands.

4

NOVEMBER

It is impossible to do nothing –
even for a moment.
For better or worse,
we are always up to something.
This compulsion to act
was impregnated in us
so that our inner consciousness
should become clearly visible
in the outer world.

5

NOVEMBER

The only reason you don't rush toward Perfection
is that you think you are already perfect.
There is no greater soul-sickness than this conceit.
The water may look pure to you,
but, let me assure you, the riverbed is covered in dung.

6

NOVEMBER

Hey, Mr Fox!
Don't perform good deeds
for secret selfish reasons.
Rush into the fire like a moth.
Don't hoard up goodness.
Let your love flow freely.

7

NOVEMBER

If you've never seen the devil take a look at yourself.

8

NOVEMBER

Lies collect around those who are living a lie.

9

NOVEMBER

Hallaj proclaimed "I am God" –
a selfless statement of Truth.
Pharaoh also declared "I am God" –
but that was an egotistical lie.

10
NOVEMBER

Someone who says he never suffers is probably a liar,
because to be without pain is to be God.

Assert "I am God" as the truth,
if you understand what you are saying.

But watch out! Make sure this isn't just empty bluster.
Cocks that crow too early get their heads cut off!

11
NOVEMBER

A conceited scholar was traveling on a boat.
"Have you ever studied books, my man?"
he asked the boatman:
"No," came the ashamed reply.
"Then your life up until now has been wasted,"
declared the scholar.

A little later, a whirlpool caught the boat in its eddies.
"Have you ever learned to swim, Sir?"
asked the boatman.
"No. I have never had time for such amusement,"
the scholar replied.
"In that case," said the boatman, "your life from now on has
been wasted, because we are about to sink."

12
NOVEMBER

If you don't know yourself to be an ass,
you certainly are an ass.

13

NOVEMBER

An intellectual struck Zaid on the neck and asked,
"Tell me this. When I hit you, there was the sound of a slap.
Was it caused by my hand or by your neck?"
Zaid replied, "Listen, friend! I'm in pain right now and not in
the mood to impartially consider this matter. You, on the
other hand, are not in pain! So I suggest you work out the
answer for yourself!"

 14

NOVEMBER

Hey! Mr Know-it-all.
Do you know where your knowledge comes from?

15

NOVEMBER

It is imagining you know what the Treasure is
that stops you seeing the Treasure.
Concepts are like plowed fields.
The Treasure is hidden where it's wild.

 16

NOVEMBER

The hunter triumphantly grabs the shadow of the bird,
while the bird on the branch looks on in amazement,
thinking to himself, "What's this blockhead cheering about?"

 17

NOVEMBER

God said to Moses, "You saw the moon rise from your chest.
I filled you with Divine Light. I am God. Yet, when I got sick,
you never visited me!"
Moses said, "Transcendent One. I don't know what you're
talking about. Please set me straight."
God repeated, "When I was sick, you never came."
Moses said, "Perfect One. You have no imperfections! I don't
understand. What are you talking about?"
God said, "One of my lovers was ill, and you ignored it.
I am him. His sickness is my sickness. Think it over."

NOVEMBER

Some people act as if they're guests at God's place
every time they stop for fuel at a spiritual service station.
You have to leave behind a lot of roadside motels
if you want to make it all the way home.

NOVEMBER

Four Indians were in a mosque, waiting in reverent silence
for prayers to begin. When the muezzin came in, one of the
Indians whispered to him, "Have you given the
call to prayer yet?"
Hearing this, the second Indian remarked, "Hey! You've spoken
when you shouldn't, so your prayers will be worthless."
The third Indian observed wryly, "Forget criticizing him –
what about yourself? You have just broken the silence as well."
At which, the fourth Indian piously announced, "I thank you,
God, that I alone have not made the error of speaking."

NOVEMBER

Don't give me this pretentious nonsense.
I'm not interested in your pompous artificiality.
Reputation is your religion.
Look at what you actually do and feel.
You should be ashamed of yourself!

21

NOVEMBER

A table of food descended from Heaven
to feed Moses and his hungry people.
No one had to work for it.
It wasn't bought or sold.
Then some people started complaining,
"Hey! Where are the garlic and lentils?"
And immediately it disappeared.

22

NOVEMBER

You are so identified with being a seeker after selflessness
that, when you come home, there's always someone in.

23

NOVEMBER

God says, "You are not in love with Me.
You are in love with the hope of getting high."

24

NOVEMBER

Are you walking out on Love
because you've been shown up as a fool?
You don't know anything about Love,
except how to say the word!

25

NOVEMBER

Who are you trying to run from?
Yourself?
That's impossible!

26

NOVEMBER

"If only I'd done that."
"If only it had turned out differently."
Don't be the prisoner of "if only."
The Prophet forbade his people to indulge in such nonsense.
He called it "hypocrisy,"
because a hypocrite's last words are "if only!"
An "if-only-life" is a life you'll live to regret.

27

NOVEMBER

Don't give up looking for the true Friend of God.
The Treasure is hidden somewhere, so search every ruin.
Select a Master at random and check him out.
If he is for real then stick with him like glue.
While you don't have inner vision,
always remember that any stranger you pass in the street
may be the custodian of the Treasure.

28

NOVEMBER

Where's the way out?
Run about wildly like a madman
looking for a secret passage –
a means of escape into the non-spatial.
You came into the world,
(although you don't know how),
so there must be a way out again.

Eventually we'll all exit through that way-less Way.
In dreams you wander happily in the land of the free,
but you have no idea how you got there.
Close your outer eyes and give up,
then you will find yourself in the ancient city of Reality.

29

NOVEMBER

You struggle within me like an embryo.
Please make it easy for me to give birth
or give up on me altogether.
Since You're demanding gold from a bankrupt,
You'd better slip me some money in secret.

30

NOVEMBER

Don't look so sour.
Thousands of happy souls
have made it
to the ocean of honey.

WINTER

SWIMMING IN AN OCEAN OF ALLAH

Winter is a time for death. Do you think death is a bad thing? Then you still haven't got it. You've lived countless lives and died countless deaths in an endless process of evolution. Each death has brought you more life. Without death, there is no rebirth. The ultimate death is nothing to do with the body. It is the death of your self as separate from God. You are standing at the edge of His ocean of Love. Plunge below the surf of separation. Dive into the mystical depth. Dissolve yourself into that sea. Like a moth around a candle, be irresistibly drawn to the light until you are engulfed by flames in an inferno of communion. The lover chooses the fire because he knows the secret: "The honey is worth the sting."

DECEMBER

The Prophets are fishes swimming in an ocean of Allah.

2
DECEMBER

Those with hearts on fire
aren't enamored of scent and color.

They see Beauty itself
everywhere in every moment.

They spit out the shell of opinion
and taste the kernel of immediate experience.

They tear away thoughts
and uncover consciousness.

They cross the sea to the source of Gnosis.

3
DECEMBER

Philanthropists donate money,
but the Gnostic surrenders his soul.

If you give bread in Allah's name,
you will never know hunger.

If you give your life for Allah,
you will really feel alive.

4
DECEMBER

Every night You release the spirit
from its body-prison
and erase the mind of memory.
Each night the bird is uncaged
and the waking narrative pauses.

Prisoners aren't in prison.
Governors are powerless.
No pain or aching.
No worries about getting or losing.
No fantasies about this or that person.

This is the Gnostic's state when wide awake.

5
DECEMBER

Sleep is the brother of Death.

6
DECEMBER

The bliss of deep sleep is a free sample
of the consciousness enjoyed by the Gnostics,
even when going about their business.
Allah pulls them to Him —
they don't bother to do anything.
Without any conscious volition on their part,
they respond to Allah like an echo.

7
DECEMBER

There are many idiots who venerate mosques,
yet attack those whose hearts are the home of Allah.

8

DECEMBER

A moment of insight is the unveiling of the beautiful bride.
Permanent enlightenment is making love with her.

All the wedding guests get to see the bride unveiled,
but only her lover gets to become one with her in private.

Many Sufis have glimpsed Reality unveiled,
but few have been invited to bed.

9

DECEMBER

Muhammad saw through the smoke,
and from then on,
wherever he turned,
he saw the face of Allah.

10

DECEMBER

He is right in front of you.
But which way is that?
Where's the front of the soul?
"Front or back" refers to bodies.
The Light-Spirit is spaceless.
Explore your non-spatial interior.
Don't be a short-sighted daydreamer
confused by the nightmare of being a body.
In Reality "you" don't exist.
What have "before and behind"
got to do with non-existence?

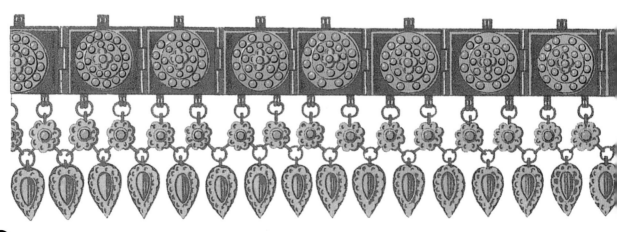

 11

DECEMBER

They say the middle path is the way of wisdom,
but it too is completely relative.
Relative to a camel, a stream is nothing,
but, to a mouse, it is an ocean.
To work out the middle,
you have to know where things start and end.
But infinity is not limited like this.
Who knows which path is in the middle?

 12

DECEMBER

Turn toward that which transcends direction.

 13

DECEMBER

You can't see Spirit
because it's so close.

14

DECEMBER

Your form is now-here.
Your Spirit is nowhere.

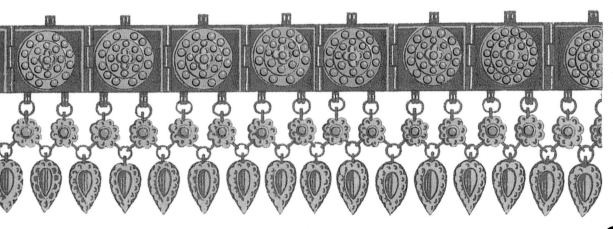

15
DECEMBER

Shut up shop in Somewhere City –
it's only a temporary residence.

Open shop in Nowheresville –
your original home before you were born.

17
DECEMBER

Form springs from Spirit-Reality
like a lion from the jungle.

Form springs from Spirit-Reality
like speech from thought.

16
DECEMBER

Forms come from formlessness
and then go back again.

As the saying has it,
"Truly we are returning to Him."

18
DECEMBER

Speech comes from thought,
but where do thoughts come from?

DECEMBER

All you can think of will pass away.
The unthinkable is Allah.

DECEMBER

Thoughts are confusing.
I enjoy thinking myself,
but when I want to escape,
I soar upward like a bird.
Thoughts are like gnats.
I fly down and eat them up.

DECEMBER

This world is one thought in the Universal Mind.

22

DECEMBER

A consciousness empty of appearances
is immediately ushered into the entrance lobby,
and offered an audience with the Presence.

23

DECEMBER

Whenever you think you know who you are,
run away from that self-image
and embrace Him of whom nothing can be said.

24

DECEMBER

Listen, friend. You aren't "you."
There is a mighty YOU which is an ocean
in which have drowned a billion "yous."

25

DECEMBER

You appear to be undressed in the hot tub,
but you are still clothed in appearances.
In this world everyone's in fancy dress.
Strip naked and plunge into the bath of Reality,
because you won't be let in wearing that!

26

DECEMBER

Don't wear clothes
when you're in bed
with your Loved One.

27

DECEMBER

Smile and put His gun to your head,
so that your soul will be always laughing,
like Muhammad with the Divine One.

28
DECEMBER

In a mystical vision,
the Friend appeared
to me as Abraham —
an image
of a destroyer of images.
Thank Allah
that when this phantom appeared to me,
I recognized immediately,
as if in a mirror,
that I too was an illusion.

29
DECEMBER

Hey! You who are slowly decomposing
in the garden of growth and decay,
don't you know that your everlasting soul
didn't sprout from anything —
because it was never born?

30
DECEMBER

The one you call the lover
is actually the Beloved.
He is both this and that.

31
DECEMBER

The Beloved is All.
The lover is just a corpse.

JANUARY

You – the soul free from "me" and "you."
You – the essence in every man and woman.
When the sexes become one, You are that union.
You created this business of "me" and "you,"
so that You could play the game of wooing Yourself.

JANUARY

Why worry about past, present, and future?
You are the eternal Consciousness of Allah.
Past and future exist only for a separate person
who thinks they are somewhere–sometime.

JANUARY

We name something according to how it looks.
God names something according to its essential nature.
Moses called his walking stick "staff,"
but God called it "serpent."
Umar was called "idolater,"
but God knew his name was "believer."
What we call "seed," God calls
"that which is beside me already."
It's like this – our end is our real name with God.

4

JANUARY

A man asked a goldsmith, "Please let me have some scales,
I want to weigh some gold."
The goldsmith replied, "Sorry, I don't have a sieve."
"I don't want a sieve. I said scales, you fool,"
responded the man.
"Sorry, I don't have a broom either," said the goldsmith.
"Stop this nonsense," said the man.
"Are you actually listening to me?"
"I heard you well enough and I am no fool,"
said the goldsmith. "I can see that you are a trembling old man.
Your hands shake so much that you will end up spilling the
gold when you put it on the scales. This gold of yours is a fine
powder, so you will then ask me for a broom.
When you sweep up, you will have both dust and gold, and
you will ask me for a sieve to separate them.
You see, I saw the end from the beginning."

5

JANUARY

Beyond the world of opposites
birth and maturity are one.

Thousands of years
are the same as a single hour.

Time and eternity
are reflections of each other.

6

JANUARY

The Beloved is the One
that has no beginning and no end.
When you find Him,
you'll desire nothing else.
He is both the manifest and the Mystery.

JANUARY

The One appears to be many to the cross-eyed
who can only see things through the spectacles of duality.

JANUARY

Every moment millions of opposites
are mutually annihilating each other,
and then mutually recreating each other.
There is a continual stream of traffic
driving between non-being and being.

Each night all thoughts dissolve
into the dark sea of nothingness,
but the dawn drags them up
from the depths like fishes.

Autumn loots the life from the world,
and the crow mourns in his black suit and tie.
But Spring recovers the stolen goodness.
My friend, think about this for a second –
Autumn and Spring are always within you.

JANUARY

Love and strife got married and parented the world.

JANUARY

Life is the harmony of contraries.
Death is the conflict of complimentaries.

11
JANUARY

Brine and fresh water
are forever divided
in this world.

Leave both behind.
Go all the way
to their Source.

12
JANUARY

Until poison or sugar are the same to you,
you won't catch the scent of Oneness.

13
JANUARY

Both good and evil come from the One Cause.

14
JANUARY

Does evil come from God?
Yes, but this is not some sort of defect.
Evil is part of His perfection.
Let me explain this with a parable.
A master painter can portray both beauty and ugliness.
If he paints the ugliest picture you have ever seen,
it doesn't mean that he is ugly –
only that he has limitless talent.
If he could only paint pretty things,
he wouldn't be a great painter.
Do you see what I'm trying to get at?

JANUARY

Everything in this world eats and is eaten.
Those who understand Allah accept this.

In this world all journeys end in tragedy,
but in the other world we journey on forever.

In this world lovers are inevitably parted,
but in the other they are eternally united.

JANUARY

All these lovely things are trivial
compared with the deep Sea.

Forget the parts.
Fix your gaze upon the Whole.

JANUARY

The one sun refracts into myriad rays
when it passes through a window.

The One Spirit fractures into myriad forms
when it passes through the world.

JANUARY

Many moons seem to shimmer
in the mirror of the old pond,
but, in reality,
only one moon shines in an empty space.

19

JANUARY

LOVE.
Destroyer of difference.
Revealer of Oneness.

JANUARY

You wouldn't be able to see red or green
or gold without light.
But you're so dazzled by colors that they've
become a light-shade.

Without light there are no colors.
If you don't believe me try seeing them in the dark.

JANUARY

The miracle is color from colorlessness.

JANUARY

When a lamp has been lit from a candle,
seeing the lamplight is seeing the candlelight.
If a hundred lamps are lit one from the other,
seeing the last is seeing the first.

JANUARY

Immature grapes are made ripe by the breath of the Master.
Then the sourness of duality, hate, and strife disappears,
and they are peeled of their skins to become one in the wine.

JANUARY

We have experienced
a billion rebirths.
From inanimate matter,
we unconsciously evolved
into vegetable consciousness.
And then into animal life
with all of its associated troubles.
And then onward
to rationality
and moral discernment.
And then further
to intuitive awareness
of what lies beyond
the evidence of the senses.
Footprints extend
as far as the shore.
Beyond that they disappear
into the Ocean.

25
JANUARY

The ocean of Consciousness is wide
and our forms bob on its surface
like empty cups,
until we become full with its waters,
and then we sink to its depths.

26
JANUARY

Do you want to drown in God?
Then submerge yourself.
Don't bob up and down
like flotsam on the sea
wondering, "Which is preferable –
the depths or the surface?"

27
JANUARY

Those lovers who are near to the Beloved
are moths irresistibly drawn to a burning candle.

28
JANUARY

Nothing is certain until you burn.
Do you want to know for sure?
Then sit down by the fire.

If this is Your fire,
what must Your light be like?
If this is Your wake,
I can't wait for Your wedding day.
You're bitterly beautiful
and severely sweet.
I complain all the time,
but please don't listen.
Don't dampen the flames with kindness.
I delight in Your violence
as well as Your gentleness.
It's astonishing
that I can want these contraries.
If I ever make it to the Garden of Joy,
I shall moan like a nightingale,
missing feasting
on both sweet and savory.
What a strange bird!
Not a bird but a fiery dragon,
who cooks with fire
until everything tastes of Love.

Love is a flame which consumes everything but the Beloved.

The lover strafes the world with "NOT"
like shots from a machine-gun –
Ratter-tat-tat! Ratter-tat-tat!
Not this! Not that! Not this! Not that!
Not! Not! Not-Not-Not!
When he has eliminated everything he can think of,
God is the One wearing the bulletproof vest.

1

FEBRUARY

The lover said to his Beloved,
"I have worked hard
to buy you the best of everything.
Now I'm broke and exhausted."

He didn't drink these bitter dregs
to boast or complain,
but to stoke the embers
of the irrational fire
which burned inside him.

His Beloved replied,
"All this time, I have never asked you
for all these bouquets of devotion.
Just give me yourself.
If you want to live for Me,
then die to 'you.'"

Laughing with relief,
the lover lay down
and gave himself away.
He entered the eternal laughter.
His heart became tranquil.
His intelligence became transparent.
He became one of the Gnostics.

2

FEBRUARY

To be washed in Allah
is to be baptized
in a vat of dye,
which magically makes
all colored cloth
turn colorless.

FEBRUARY

The mystic plunged into the vat.
Someone called, "Come on out. You're done."
He replied in rapture, "How can I?
I am the vat! I can't do anything."

FEBRUARY

When Umar became a mirror of the Mystery,
his old heart woke up with a start.
He quit laughing or wailing.
His soul died and a new one was born.
He was so astonished,
Heaven and Earth couldn't hold him.

I can't describe such penetration.
If you think you can do it justice, go ahead!
How do you paint the portrait of someone
who has been drowned in Beauty?
Not swimming, mark you, but completely sunken.
No one could tell him apart from the Divine Ocean.

FEBRUARY

All day parched with burning love.
All night a restless sense of separation.

Then I was abruptly blasted beyond day and night,
like a bullet through an armored vest.

6
FEBRUARY

A man knocked on the Friend's door.
"Who's there?" asked the Friend.
"It's me," said the man.
"Go away, then," said the Friend,
"There's no room here for two.
There's no place at my table for raw food."

The distraught man traveled for a year
until the fire within had cooked him.
Then he returned to the door and,
having paced up and down nervously for a while,
silently and respectfully knocked again.
"Who's there?," asked the Friend.
"Oh Charmer-of-Hearts, it's You," replied the man.
"Well come on in," said the Friend,
"Since we are One, there's room for two."

7
FEBRUARY

You've no idea
how hard I've looked for a gift to bring You.
Nothing seemed right.
What's the point of bringing gold to a gold mine,
or a jug of water to the ocean.
Everything I came up with
was like taking spices to the Orient.
It's no good giving my heart and soul,
because You already have these.
So – I've brought you a mirror.
Look at Yourself and remember me.

While we suffer from separation,
love fashions from itself a form —
something tangible we can relate to.
But in the moment of Union,
the formless One says,
"I am the Source
of seriousness and intoxication.
All beauties express My Beauty.
I am Beauty itself.
You have abandoned yourself completely
to contemplation of My reflection.
Now you have won the right
to wonder at My naked Essence."

9

FEBRUARY

Allah says to the saint,
"I am your tongue and eyes.
I am all your senses.
I am your happiness and anger.
You are my property,
but I belong to you.
Sometimes I say 'You are you.'
Other times I say 'You are Me.'
Whatever I say, I am the Sun
which brings it to light."

10

FEBRUARY

You are a sculptor and I am Your idol.
I become however you shape me.
I am a pen between Your two fingers.
I won't wobble this way and that.
I will write whatever you want to say.

11

FEBRUARY

Ignorance is His prison and Knowledge His palace.
If we stay asleep, we are His drunks.
If we wake up, we are His hands.
When weeping, we rain His bounty,
When laughing, we crack His lightning.
In anger, we reflect His power.
In forgiveness, we express His Love.
Lost in this tangled world — who are we?
What is there apart from Him? Nothing.

12

FEBRUARY

I have abandoned everything but You.
When I died into You, I became You.

13

FEBRUARY

When you have attained Union,
you don't need a go-between.
When you have found what you are looking for,
searching becomes a waste of time.
When you have reached the highest Heaven,
you don't go and buy a ladder.
When you are happy,
you're not interested in how you got there,
except to help others to travel.

14

FEBRUARY

I am a lover of the Universal.
I am the Universal Lover.
I am You in love with Yourself.
I am You seeking your own Love.

15

FEBRUARY

I finally found myself in selflessness.

16

FEBRUARY

Whatever scrapes this body gets itself into,
I am the Witness watching at the window.

17

FEBRUARY

I exist in a place beyond the reach of thoughts.

FEBRUARY

My wings have grown out of my essential nature –
they're not stuck on with glue.

FEBRUARY

Unless you visit for yourself,
you will suspect that I live in La-La Land.
Only someone who lives at the spiritual horizon
knows that this is Reality.

FEBRUARY

Don't become a Sufi
to avoid getting entangled with the world.
Sufis understand that nothing exists but Allah.

FEBRUARY

To you it's a prison, but to me it's a garden.
To me, involvement with the world
has become spiritual freedom.
Your feet squelch in the mud,
but my mud is mulch for roses.
You are mourning while I beat the drum.
I may be living with you here on Earth,
but I also occupy galaxies beyond Saturn.
In fact, I'm not sitting here beside you at all –
that's only my shadow.

25

FEBRUARY

This is the secret
You have shared with Your angels:

"The honey is worth the sting."

26

FEBRUARY

Not united.
Not separate.
Just perfect.

22

FEBRUARY

You are not a product of my imagination.
I am a product of Your imagination.

I have made up endless fables about You,
but in reality I am a character in Your novel.

23

FEBRUARY

I have told so many tall tales.
Now I realize that I myself am a fiction,
as improbable as any fairy story.

24

FEBRUARY

When we finally come home
we will laugh and laugh
at what fools we have been.

27

FEBRUARY

Don't ask me to do anything.
I've lost myself completely.
I no longer know what's what.
I can't sing or recite.
I could be piously reserved,
or exaggerate wildly,
but anything I utter
is utterly inappropriate.
When I am absent
I don't even have a body,
so how can I paint pictures
of the perfect Friend for you?
We'll have to leave that for another time.

28

FEBRUARY

Mystical bewilderment
is a beautiful bird
perched on your head.
You don't want to breathe
for fear you will disturb it.
And if anyone says anything,
you put a finger to your mouth
and whisper "Shhhh!!"

29

FEBRUARY

I was reciting love poems to my Beloved,
full of longing and desire to be with her.
She interrupted,
"Don't you think it's a waste
of our precious time together
to be reading these poems now?
I am sitting here beside you.
Make love to me – don't talk about it."

BY THE SAME AUTHOR

Encyclopedia of Spirituality
Shamanic Wisdomkeepers
Illustrated Sacred Scriptures
The Wisdom of the Sufi Sages
The Wisdom of the Christian Mystics
The Wisdom of the Hindu Gurus
The Wisdom of the Tibetan Lamas
The Wisdom of the Zen Masters
Zen Wisdom
Zen Koan Card Pack
Zen Made Easy
Taoist Wisdom
Lao Tzu's Tao Te Ching
The Way of the Sea
The Way of the Desert
The Principle of Native American Spirituality
(co-author Wa'Na'Nee'Che')

BOOKS CO-AUTHORED WITH PETER GANDY

The Jesus Mysteries
— Was The "Original" Jesus a Pagan God?
The Complete Guide to World Mysticism
The Hermetica — The Lost Wisdom of the Pharaohs
The Wisdom of the Pagan Philosophers

To find out more about Timothy Freke,
his books, lectures and weekend seminars,
visit his website, www.timfreke.demon.co.uk,
or write to PO Box 2638, Glastonbury,
Somerset, BA6 9WF, England.